The Start Up Yearbook

A guide to document your start-up journey

Christine Michaelis

Copyright © 01.04.2017 Christine Michaelis

All rights reserved. No part of this book may be reproduced, stored in a retrieval system, or transmitted, in any form or by any means, electronic, mechanical, photocopying, recording or otherwise, without the prior written permission of the copyright owner.

ISBN-13: 978-1979001847
ISBN-10: 1979001847

ENDORSEMENTS

"The Start-Up Yearbook is perfect for anyone just starting out in business as well as for anyone already established as most of the daily inspirational quotes, tips and to dos are simple guides that help you on your journey and keep you motivated along the way. So this is perfect for anyone who has their own business. Being self-employed can be a daunting thing and Christine makes it very easy for you to prioritise your to dos, give you space to scribble down your thoughts and take away the overwhelming feeling that you can easily feel whilst on this journey. And as always with her quirky and refreshing style she included lots of fun and cute little doodle to turn this book into something truly special. The perfect thing about this book is that you can start using the yearbook whenever you start your journey, so you are not bound to the calendar year as with most planners. I've been a business owner myself for several years already, but handling the day-to-day and planning for taking your business to the next level are very much the same whether you are just starting out or not, so I will definitely get myself a copy when it comes out – can't wait! Thank you, Christine, for creating something so wonderful and useful the same."

Magdalena Mahdy – Director & Owner of the Rise & Shine Society – www.riseandshinesociety.com

ENDORSEMENTS

"Christine is a true professional and her knowledge, experience and work ethic really comes to life in the pages of this book. So very practical and informative. A 'must have' by your side whether you are starting up a business or just want a more organised life style."

Marcia Baldry – Entrepreneurship Support Manager
Anglia Ruskin University

"As an enterprise educator for many years at the University of Kent I have engaged with a wide range of students, staff and alumni who wish to explore starting a business. The ideas presented often incredibly varied cutting across a whole range of sectors. What Christine has produced in The Start-Up Yearbook is a simple way of breaking down what some find the daunting task of starting a business into handy weekly sections, that regardless of sector each step absolutely applies to you and your new business. This take it a step at a time approach allows the reader to tackle each element and reflect accordingly. A tremendous compliment to her existing range of books already available to the entrepreneurs out there!"

Marcus Wright, Enterprise Relationship Manager,
University of Kent

 DEDICATION

I dedicate this book to my **family** - my mum, my dad and my sister – who have always inspired and supported me in all my adventures. Because of them I don't give up. Thank you. I love you.

ACKNOWLEDGEMENTS

Thank you to **Hayley Jones** for proofreading my book and checking it over.

Thank you to my friend **Magda** who has helped me throughout my start-up journey with valuable advice and input. www.riseandshinesociety.com

Also thank you to another one of my dear friends **Taz** who supported me in many ways in my adventures. Thank you. www.vercossa.com

I also would like to acknowledge **all the start-ups** I have worked with. Working with them has helped me in shaping products and creating valuable resources for you – including this book.

HOW IT WORKS

This book is divided into **52 weeks**. Each week has a specific topic and will have the following content:

- An inspirational **quote**
- A section named **'The 1 thing'** in which I want you to write down the 1 thing you can do this week to move your start-up towards your goal
- A **tip** related to the topic of the week
- A **challenge** of the week to develop your start-up and skills
- An **inspiration for** the week
- An outline of **additional material** that you can download for more info
- **Space** for writing down thoughts, notes of mentoring sessions etc.

The **banner** at the top of each week is meant for you to **put in the date of the week**. This way you can start your year any time and are not bound to the calendar year.

As mentioned above, every week comes with **additional material** that you can download in case you want to dive deeper into the topic. You can download all material here:
www.startup-yearbook.com/material

After 52 weeks you will **have your own Start-Up Yearbook** documenting a year of your start-up journey :-) I am looking forward to supporting you.

Your Marketing and Creative Start-Up Coach
Christine

WEEK 1 - GOAL SETTING

"It's not about ideas. It's about making ideas happen." Scott Belsky

Defining a goal helps you to create an action plan.

 The 1 thing

Tip: Set long term goals but break them down into manageable chunks

Inspiration
http://bit.ly/tsygoal

Challenge of the week:
Set yourself a long-term goal using the following acronym: **ACHIEVE** (see also additional material)

- As if it **already happened**
- Putting **specifics** in such as location, date, turnover etc.
- Check if you can actually **achieve it**
- State what you want using **positive language** rather than stating what you don't want
- Is this **your** goal? Is it **exciting** for you?
- Can you **verify** when you have achieved your goal?
- Who around you is **effected** when you achieved your goal?

Your goal:

Your week was
- ☐ a sunset
- ☐ a sunrise
- ☐ cloudy with a chance of sunshine

Additional material:
ACHIEVE goal setting acronym
www.startup-yearbook.com/material

Space for notes:

WEEK 2 - VALUES

"When your values are clear to you, making decisions becomes easier." Roy E. Disney

Knowing your values helps you with business decisions.

The 1 thing

Challenge of the week:

Make a list of what is important to you in your business and define your top 10 values.

Tip: Once you defined your values, write them down and communicate them so that people get a better understanding what your startup stands for.

Space for doodle:

Inspiration
http://bit.ly/tsyvalues

What is important to you?

Your top 10 values

1. 6.

2. 7.

3. 8.

4. 9.

5. 10.

>────────────────────────────────<

Your week was
- ☐ smiley face
- ☐ sad face
- ☐ suspicious face

>────────────────────────────────<

Additional material:
Examples of values
www.startup-yearbook.com/material

>────────────────────────────────<

Space for notes:

WEEK 3 - YOUR VISION 🔭

"Don't be cocky. Don't be flashy. There's always someone better than you." Tony Hsieh

Knowing your vision helps you to know where you are going.

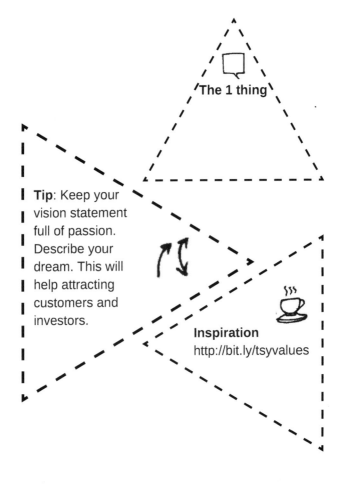

The 1 thing

Tip: Keep your vision statement full of passion. Describe your dream. This will help attracting customers and investors.

Inspiration
http://bit.ly/tsyvalues

Challenge of the week: Write your vision statement. Use these questions to help you: What are you selling? What is the company's image? Where will you be located? Where will your customers be? Who are you? Who is your customer? When will you be operating? Why are you doing this? Why would anyone invest in you? How do you want to interact?

Your vision statement:

Your week was
- [ ] a whistle
- [ ] a yodel
- [ ] a song

Additional material:
Examples of vision statements
www.startup-yearbook.com/material

Space for notes:

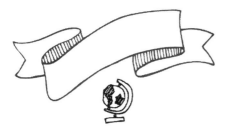

WEEK 4 - YOUR MISSION

"Be the change you want to see in the world" Gandhi

Knowing your mission helps you to keep motivated.

The 1 thing

 Tip: Keep your mission statement concise. This is your purpose, not about money.

Inspiration: http://bit.ly/tsymission

Space for doodle:

Challenge of the week:

Write your mission statement.

Think about your Unique Selling Point (USP).

Who is your ideal customer?

What are the benefits to the customer?

What will your impact be?

Your mission statement:

Your week was

- [ ] loud
- [ ] mute
- [ ] just right

Additional material:
Mission statement examples
www.startup-yearbook.com/material

Space for notes:

WEEK 5 - IDEAL CLIENT

"Make something people want —
including making a company that people
want to work for." Sahil Lavingi

Knowing your ideal client helps you to target them easier.

The 1 thing

Tip

It is not only important to know who you want to sell to but also who you want to work with.

Space for doodle:

Inspiration

http://bit.ly/tsyclient

Challenge

Define your ideal client. Start with the following questions:
What kind of people do you like to be around?
Who would benefit most from your products and services? Where can you find those people?

Write down your ideal client (see also additional material for an example):

Notes:

Your week was

- ☐ blowing a kiss
- ☐ slapping someone's face
- ☐ a hug

Material

Additional material:
Sample ideal client definition
www.startup-yearbook.com/material

Notes:

WEEK 6 - MOTIVATION

"Your most unhappy customers are your greatest source of learning." Bill Gates

Knowing what motivates you helps you to know what to do when things don't go as planned.

The 1 thing

....

Tip

People are motivated by different things. Some are motivated by **getting away** from something; some are motivated by **going towards** something. What language are YOU using? Are you trying to get towards or away from something?

....

Inspiration
http://bit.ly/tsymotivation

....

Space for doodle:

Challenge of the week:

What motivates you in life?
Write down at least 3 things.

....
....
....
....
....
....
....
....
....
....
....
....

Your week was: ☐ mind blowing

☐ easy going

☐ a battle

Additional material:
Examples of what motivates people
www.startup-yearbook.com/material

Space for notes:

WEEK 7 - WHAT CAN HELP

"It's simple until you make it complicated."
Jason Fried

Knowing what can help you supports you to achieve your goal quicker.

The 1 thing

Tip

Knowing what skills and equipment you need, will help you to achieve your goal and move forward with your business.

Inspiration

http://bit.ly/tsywhat

Challenge

Make a list of all the skills you need to improve or acquire. What equipment do you need (hardware, software etc.)?

Your week was

- [ ] closing the deal
- [ ] paradise
- [ ] the desert

Additional material

Overview of entrepreneurial skill set
www.startup-yearbook.com/material

Space for notes:

WEEK 8 - WHO CAN HELP

"If you don't ask, you don't get."
Stevie Wonder

Knowing who can help you will move your business forward quicker.

The 1 thing

Tip

Not only know what can help you but who can help you to achieve your goals.

Inspiration

http://bit.ly/tsyconnection

Challenge

Who can help you with moving your business forward? Family, friends, experts, previous teachers, networking group... List them below.

Who can help you?

Your week was

- [ ] a fruit
- [ ] a flower
- [ ] bread

Additional material

Examples of people that can help you.

Space for notes:

WEEK 9 - ACCOMPLISHMENTS

"A goal is a dream with a deadline."
Napoleon Hill

Acknowledging your accomplishments helps to stay motivated.

The 1 thing

Tip

Accomplishments can be big or small. You should always celebrate them. That will keep you even more motivated.

Inspiration

http://bit.ly/tsyaccomplishment

Space for doodle:

Challenge of the week:

What accomplishments would you like to achieve this year? Next year? Where do the accomplishments come from and what do they look like? How will you celebrate them?

Your week was ☐ sexy

☐ boring

☐ strong

Additional material:

Accomplishement worksheet
www.startup-yearbook.com/material

Space for notes:

WEEK 10 – DIGITAL DETOX

"Either you run the day or the day runs you."
Jim Rohn

Digital detox can bring great inspiration.

The 1 thing

Tip: Having a digital detox – even just for a day will help your mind to focus again and will make space for new ideas.

Inspiration
http://bit.ly/tsydigitaldetox

Challenge of the week: Do a digital detox this week – for as long as you can but at least for 1 day.

Space for doodles and other offline thoughts:

Your week was:

☐ a yoga retreat

☐ a circus

☐ a festival

Additional material: Tips for digital detox.
www.startup-yearbook.com/material

Space for notes:

WEEK 11 - PLANNING

"Don't let yesterday take up too much of today."
Will Rogers

When planning things, you will feel less stressed.

The 1 thing

Tip

 Dedicating each day of the week to a different topic, will help you focus on one thing at a time.

Inspiration

http://bit.ly/tsyplan

Challenge

Plan a sample week by dividing each day into blocks (morning, afternoon, evening) that you allocate tasks/topics to.

$a^2 + b^2 = c^2$

Your week was

☐ a winner

☐ a runner up

☐ cosi cosi

Additional material

Download planner templates at
www.startup-yearbook.com/material

Space for notes

WEEK 12 - POSITIVE LANGUAGE

"Creativity is intelligence having fun."
Albert Einstein

Positive language will have a positive effect on your life.

The 1 thing

Tip

Changing your language to positive language, will change your mind to positive thinking and will show you more opportunities in life.

Inspiration
http://bit.ly/tsypositive

Challenge

Analyse your language and see if you can turn negative words into positive words.

Negative words	Turned into positive words

Your week was:

☐ a kettle

☐ a toaster

☐ a fridge

Additional material:
Examples of positive language
How to turn negatives into positives

Space for notes

WEEK 13 - LIMITING BELIEFS

"Do or do not. There is no try."
Yoda

Limiting beliefs hold you back. Knowing them helps you to overcome them.

> **The 1 thing**

Tip: The first step to overcome an obstacle is to discover what is holding you back. What 'limiting belief' do you hold that you need to challenge?

Inspiration
http://bit.ly/tsybelief

Challenge of the week:
Write down your limiting beliefs and understand why you have them. What caused this belief? Is it real?

Space for doodle:

Your week was

- [ ] simple
- [ ] ideal
- [ ] a plastic cup

Additional material:
Limiting belief worksheet
www.startup-yearbook.com/material

Space for notes:

Week 14 – Work Environment

"It's not that we don't need new ideas, but we need to stop having old ideas." Edwin Land

Changing your work environment helps to open your mind to new things.

The 1 thing

>————————————<

Tip: Changing your work environment on a regular basis, will make it more stimulating and will open up your brain to new ways of thinking.

>————————————<

Inspiration
http://bit.ly/tsyworkspace

Challenge of the week: Change your work environment this week. Can you put new postcards, pictures, quotes, posters up? Can you have fresh flowers? Change the colours around you?

>————————————<

Space for doodle:

List things you can change in your work environment

Even more space for doodle:

>————————————————————<

Your week was
- [ ] a marathon
- [ ] doing push-ups
- [ ] a journey

>————————————————————<

Additional material:
Examples of what you can use to
change your work environment
www.startup-yearbook.com/material

>————————————————————<

Space for notes:

Week 15 - Feedback Scrapbook

"Always deliver more than expected."
Larry Page

A Feedback Scrapbook helps you to capture positive feedback to stay motivate.

The 1 thing

Tip: When you are feeling down, it helps to remember the things that went well and the positive feedback that you received.

Inspiration
http://bit.ly/tsyfeedback

Challenge of the week:
Create a feedback scrapbook
Online or offline
Look back what you can put in it already. When was the last time you received positive feedback about your work?

Brainstorm good feedback you received in the past that you can add to your scrapbook

Your week was
- [ ] a doodle
- [ ] a Picasso
- [ ] a photo

Additional material:
How to create a feedback scrapbook, what apps, software/ books can you use?
www.startup-yearbook.com/material

Space for notes:

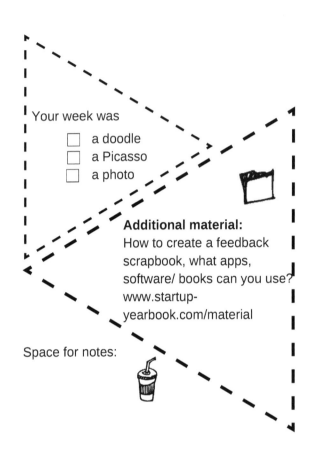

WEEK 16 - TACKLE YOUR BIGGEST CHALLENGE

"Every problem has a solution. You just need to be creative to find it."
Travis Kalanick

Tackling your biggest challenge will clear your mind for new things.

The 1 thing

Tip: Breaking big challenges down into smaller tasks will help you tackle them easier. It will give you clarity on how to solve them.

Inspiration: http://bit.ly/tsysteps

Space for doodle:

Challenge of the week:

What is your biggest challenge right now?

How can you break it down into single tasks?

Who can help you solving it?

What can help you solving it?

Answers to the questions above:

Your week was

- [ ] an action movie
- [ ] a comedy
- [ ] a romantic movie

Additional material: breaking it down into chunks worksheet
www.startup-yearbook.com/material

Space for notes:

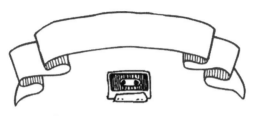

WEEK 17 - PRODUCTIVITY PLAYLIST

"The way to get started is to quit talking and begin doing." Walt Disney

Creating a productivity playlist will make you more efficient.

The 1 thing

Tip

Music can work as an 'anchor'. Listening to the same music when working, can programme your brain for productivity.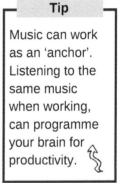

Space for doodle:

Inspiration

http://bit.ly/tsyanchor

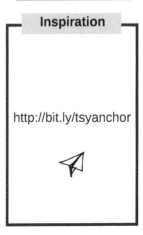

Challenge

Create a productivity playlist and listen to it when you are most productive and working well. Your brain will then get into this productivity mindset when it hears the playlist.

Write down what you are listening to when you are most productive:

Notes:

Your week was

☐ a post it note

☐ a magazine

☐ a book

Material

Spotify productivity playlists
www.startup-yearbook.com/material

Notes:

Week 18 - Future Interview

"Mistakes will not end your business. If you are nimble and willing to listen to constructive criticism you can excel by learning and evolving."
Meridith Valiando Rojas

Looking back helps you to see solutions.

The 1 thing

....

Tip

Looking at the present from the future, can help you to identify how to overcome challenges.

....

Inspiration
http://bit.ly/tsyfuture

....

Space for doodle:

Challenge of the week:
The Future interview. Pretend you are giving an interview in the future about your start-up journey. Talk about the challenges and how you overcame them. What went well? What didn't work out? (see also additional material)

....
....
....
....
....
....
....
....
....
....
....
....

Your week was: ☐ an evergreen

♫ ☐ a one hit wonder

☐ a big hit

Additional material:
The future interview questions
www.startup-yearbook.com/material

Space for notes:

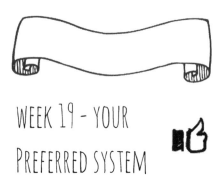

Week 19 – Your Preferred System

"Trust your instincts." Estee Lauder

Knowing your preferred system will change the way you work.

The 1 thing

Tip

Knowing what makes you most productive and what works best for you will move you forward quicker.

Inspiration

http://bit.ly/tsypattern

Challenge

Analyse your current working pattern/system. Try new things and see what happens. Play. Optimise your way of working and make it perfect. List new things you can try out.

Your week was

- [ ] a slow dance
- [ ] a salsa dance
- [ ] wrecking

 Additional material

Examples of apps, books etc. that can make you more productive
www.startup-yearbook.com/material

Space for notes:

WEEK 20 - DO SOMETHING YOU ARE REALLY AFRAID OF

"I knew that if I failed I wouldn't regret it, but I knew the one thing I might regret is not trying." Jeff Bezos

Facing your fears helps you to experience freedom.

The 1 thing

Tip

Pushing your boundries and facing your fear will make you less fearful and opens up new opportunities.

Inspiration

http://bit.ly/tsyfear

Challenge: Do one thing that you are afraid of doing (bungee jump, petting a dog — anything as big or small as it seems). List things below.

What are you afraid of?

Your week was

- [ ] holding a snake
- [ ] petting a koala
- [ ] watching kittens

Additional material

Examples of what people are afraid of

Space for notes:

WEEK 21 - BODY LANGUAGE

"Knowing is not enough; we must apply.
Willing is not enough; we must do."
Johann Wolfgang von Goethe

Body language is a main factor in communication.

The 1 thing

Tip

Being aware of your and other people's body language will improve communication between all parties.

Inspiration

http://bit.ly/tsybody

Space for doodle:

Challenge of the week:

Watch your body language and adjust it to other people's body language to see how that improves the communication between you.

Thoughts:

Your week was
- ☐ on hold
- ☐ no signal
- ☐ constant ringing

Additional material:

Body language matching and mirroring, pacing and leading explained
www.startup-yearbook.com/material

Space for notes:

WEEK 22 - LISTEN TO EVERYONE

"Wonder what your customer really wants? Ask. Don't tell." Lisa Stone

Listening to everyone helps to improve your products/services.

The 1 thing

Tip: Listening to EVERYONE will help trigger new ideas in your mind.

Inspiration
http://bit.ly/tsyactivelistening

Challenge of the week: Talk to a child this week explaining to her/him your business idea. The child will ask questions that no one else will have asked you before.

Space for doodle and other thoughts:

Your week was:

- [ ] a hot air balloon
- [ ] a sky dive
- [ ] a sailing tour

Additional material:
Examples of people to talk to about your idea
www.startup-yearbook.com/material

~~~~~~~~~~~~~~~~

Space for notes:
~~~~~~~~~~~~~~~~

WEEK 23 - ELEVATOR PITCH

"I am all for conversations, but you need to have a message." Renee Blodgett

Creating an elevator pitch helps you to connect easier.

The 1 thing

Tip

Being able to convey what you are doing in an understandable, concise way is key for people to want to work with you.

Inspiration

http://bit.ly/tsypitch

Challenge of the week

Create your perfect 60 second elevator pitch and tell it to someone who doesn't know what you are doing. See if they understand or if they have questions afterwards. See also additional material for the structure.

Write down your elevator pitch below

Your week was

- [ ] a winner
- [ ] a runner up
- [ ] cosi cosi

Additional material

Download planner templates at
www.startup-yearbook.com/material

Space for notes

WEEK 24 – BE KIND

"I want to do one thing and I want to do it well."
Jan Koum
When you are kind to others, they will be kind to you.

 The 1 thing

→ **Tip**

Being kind to yourself and others will cultivate happiness.

Inspiration
http://bit.ly/tsykind

Challenge of the week

Be kind to someone that you don't know.
Do one kind thing this week.

List small acts of kindness that you will do:

Your week was:

☐   a lift

☐   a ladder

☐   stairs

Additional material:
Examples of kindness acts
www.startup-yearbook.com/material

Space for notes

WEEK 25 - THE 1 APP

"It is not the strongest of the species that survive, nor the most intelligent, but the most responsive to change."
Charles Darwin

Become more productive by using technology.

 The 1 thing

Tip: Technology is evolving very fast. New apps and other digital products are launched every day. Use technology to your advantage.

Inspiration
http://bit.ly/tsytechnology

Challenge of the week:
Find one app for your phone or computer that will make something easier in your life.

Space for doodle:

Your week was

- [ ] a thunderstorm
- [ ] a holiday
- [ ] nothing special

Additional material:
Sample apps that make things easier
www.startup-yearbook.com/material

Space for notes:

WEEK 26 - TESTIMONIAL

"What helps people, helps business."
Leo Burnett

Word of mouth is a powerful marketing tool.

The 1 thing

Tip: One of the best marketing tools is word of mouth. Let people become your fans and let them tell others about your offer.

Challenge of the week:

Who can you get a testimonial from? Where can you use these testimonials?

Space for doodles:

Inspiration
http://bit.ly/tsytestimonial

List people you can ask for testimonials:

Even more space for doodle:

>―――――――――――――――――――――――――――<

Your week was
- [ ] 24/7
- [ ] 9 to 5
- [ ] an evening stroll

>―――――――――――――――――――――――――――<

Additional material:
How to get great testimonials
www.startup-yearbook.com/material

>―――――――――――――――――――――――――――<

Space for notes:

WEEK 27 - TAKING 'ME' TIME

"There's nothing wrong with staying small.
You can do big things with a small team."
Jason Fried

Taking care of yourself is a major factor to increase your well-being.

The 1 thing

Tip: Taking time for yourself is very important. It will help you to recharge and be open to new ideas.

Inspiration
http://bit.ly/stymetime

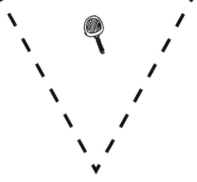

Challenge of the week:
Make time for yourself — only you, no partner, no family, no friends, no business.
Do something that you really love and do it only for yourself.

List 'me' time things you will enjoy:

Your week was
- [ ] a cake
- [ ] a dinner
- [ ] a cocktail party

Additional material:
Examples of what you can do in 'me' time
www.startup-yearbook.com/material

Space for notes:

WEEK 28 - MARKET TRENDS

"See things in the present, even if they are in the future." Larry Ellison

Knowing the market helps to see new opportunities.

The 1 thing

 Tip: Market research never ends. The world is changing faster than ever. You need to be aware of changes that are going on in your industry.

Inspiration: http://bit.ly/stytrends

Space for doodle:

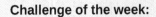

Challenge of the week:

Revisit your market research and see if you can spot a new trend.

Then adjust your products and services accordingly.

Changes you want to make in your offer:

Your week was

- [ ] productive
- [ ] creative
- [ ] enlightened

Additional material: market and competitor research document
www.startup-yearbook.com/material

Space for notes:

WEEK 29 - CHANNELS

"Opportunity is missed by most people because it is dressed in overalls and looks like work" Thomas Edison

Using different channels is an important factor for marketing success.

The 1 thing

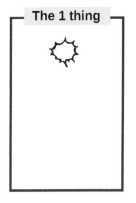

Tip

Using the right channels to reach your target audience is key. Don't waste money & time.

Space for doodle:

Inspiration

http://bit.ly/tsychannel

Challenge

Review your channels and ask yourself the following: Does this activity really reach my target audience? Did I ever get any feedback from that? Did anyone buy my product or service using this channel?

List effective channels here:

Notes:

Your week was

- ☐ a hello
- ☐ a goodbye
- ☐ a new beginning

Material

Marketing
channel examples
www.startup-
yearbook.com/material

Notes:

WEEK 30 - PRODUCT CHAIN

"Solve a real problem and the world is yours."
Aaron Patzer

Offer different products to different target groups to cater different needs.

The 1 thing

....

Tip

Using more than one medium to sell your products and services will increase your income streams.

....

Inspiration
http://bit.ly/tsyproduct

....

Space for doodle:

Challenge of the week:

What channels are you currently using to sell your products and services? List them below.

....
....
....
....
....
....
....
....
....
....
....
....

Your week was: ☐ a cucumber

☐ a strawberry

☐ a passion fruit

Additional material:
Product chain example of my products/services
www.startup-yearbook.com/material

Space for notes:

WEEK 31 - INFOGRAPHIC

"The critical ingredient is getting off your butt and doing something. It's as simple as that." Nolan Bushnell

Using infographics will increase your reach.

The 1 thing

Tip

People have different preferred ways of taking in information.

Inspiration

http://bit.ly/tsyinfographic

Challenge $a^2+b^2=c^2$

Can you create an infographic of your products and services? What is it that you offer? What are the benefits of your products/services?

Your week was

- [ ] dull
- [ ] really awful
- [ ] very interesting

Additional material

Examples of infographics
www.startup-yearbook.com/material

Space for notes:

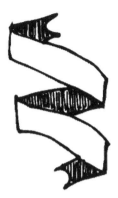

WEEK 32
CELEBRATION

"Well done is better than well said."
Benjamin Franklin

Celebrate! Starting your business will be more fun that way.

The 1 thing

Tip

You need to acknowledge your achievements and celebrate them. This will help you to stay motivated.

Inspiration

http://bit.ly/tsycelebrate

Challenge

Celebrate one of your achievements that you haven't thought of acknowledging. A small thing. Then celebrate it.

How can you celebrate?

Your week was

- [ ] a farm
- [ ] a luxury hotel
- [ ] a hostel

Additional material

Examples of how people celebrate

Space for notes:

WEEK 33 - YOUR BIG WHY

"Imagine your life is perfect in every respect; what would it look like?" Brian Tracy

Knowing your big why helps to convince other people of your cause.

The 1 thing

Tip

Knowing your 'big why' is one of the most important things. It will influence your business decisions, your mission and your motivation.

Inspiration

http://bit.ly/tsywhy

Challenge of the week:

Find or review your big why. See also additional material for questions that will help you with this.

Your why:

Your week was

- [ ] a waterfall
- [ ] a lake
- [ ] a river

Additional material:

Questions that will help you defining your big why
www.startup-yearbook.com/material

Space for notes:

WEEK 34 - BE MORE PRODUCTIVE

"The most impressive people I know spent their time with their heads down getting shit done for a long, long time." Sam Altman

Being more productive helps you to get more done.

The 1 thing

 Tip: There is always something that can be improved to be more productive

Inspiration
http://bit.ly/tsyproductivity

Challenge of the week: Try a new productivity technique that you haven't tried before.

Space for doodle and other thoughts:

Your week was:

☐ a bodybuilder

☐ a gymnast

☐ a yoga teacher

Additional material:
Productivity books
www.startup-yearbook.com/material

Space for notes:

WEEK 35 - NOT TO DO LIST

"Simple things should be simple. Complex things should be possible." Alan Kay

Knowing what not to do helps you to focus on what is important.

The 1 thing

Tip

Having a not to do list is as important as having a to do list.

Inspiration

http://bit.ly/tsynottodo

Challenge

What is it that you really don't have to and don't want to do? Take it off your to do list and put it onto your not to do list.

Your not to do list:

Your week was

- ☐ sunshine
- ☐ rain
- ☐ overcast

Additional material

 Download not to do list templates
www.startup-yearbook.com/material

Space for notes

WEEK 36 - BENEFITS

"The best start-ups generally come from somebody needing to scratch an itch."
Michael Arrington

Knowing the benefits of your products/services helps you to convince customers.

The 1 thing

Tip

When marketing your services, it is not all about the features but about the benefits.

Inspiration
http://bit.ly/tsybenefit

Challenge of the week

Write down all the benefits of your products and services for your target audience.

List benefits of your products/services:

Your week was:

☐ sightseeing

☐ a day on the beach

☐ a boat trip

Additional material:
Products/benefits worksheet
www.startup-yearbook.com/material

Space for notes

WEEK 37 - UNSUBSCRIBE

"The key ingredient to a better content experience is relevance." Jason Miller

Unsubscribe from things that you don't read, clears your inbox.

 The 1 thing

Tip: Get rid of unnecessary information to free up your time for the more important things.

Inspiration
http://bit.ly/tsyless

Challenge of the week:
Unsubscribe from the newsletters that you don't actually need or read. Make some notes which criteria are important to you to stay subscribed to a newsletter.

Space for doodle:

Your week was
- [ ] a wine tasting
- [ ] a concert
- [ ] a gym session

Additional material:
Sample criteria on how to decide which newsletter to unsubscribe from
Try unroll.me if you have a gmail account
www.startup-yearbook.com/material

Space for notes:

WEEK 38 - ACCOUNTABILITY

"In the end, a vision without the ability to
execute is probably a hallucination."
Steve Case

Accountability helps to get things done.

The 1 thing

Tip: Reporting to someone about your progress will help you to be accountable and moves you forward quicker.

Inspiration
http://bit.ly/
tsyaccountability

Challenge of the week:

Find one person that you can talk to about your goals and ask them to check with you regularly how it is going and report to them.

Space for doodle:

List people who could be your accountability partner:

Even more space for doodle:

Your week was
- [ ] past
- [ ] present
- [ ] future

Additional material:
Examples of people that you can report to.
www.startup-yearbook.com/material

Space for notes:

WEEK 39 – BE CREATIVE

"Freedom rings when you realise you can become what you never thought you could become." Richie Norton

Being creative stimulates your brain and helps to come up with new solutions.

The 1 thing

Tip: Visualising your goals and dreams will help you to achieve them.

Inspiration
http://bit.ly/tsyvisionboard

Challenge of the week:
Create a visionboard for
one of your goals.
Have a look at the additional
material to see how it's done and
examples of visionboards

Which goal do you choose to
create a visionboard for?

Your week was

- [ ] the top of the mountain
- [ ] the bottom of the sea
- [ ] a flight

Additional material:
Visionboard examples and instructions
www.startup-yearbook.com/material

Space for notes:

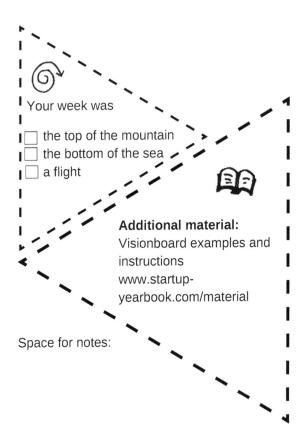

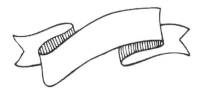

WEEK 40 - YOUR PREFERRED REPRESENTATIVE SYSTEM 👍

"To begin, begin." William Wordsworth

Knowing your preferred representative system helps to communicate better.

The 1 thing

 Tip: Everyone has a preferred language pattern. To communicate better, learn about other people's language and adjust yours to theirs.

Inspiration: http://bit.ly/tsysystem

Space for doodle:

Challenge of the week:

Find out what your preferred language pattern is.

Which words do you tend to use?

See also additional material for more explanation.

List words that indicate which language pattern you are using:

Your week was

- [ ] funny
- [ ] agreeable
- [ ] ridiculous

 Additional material: Language patterns explained/examples
www.startup-yearbook.com/material

Space for notes:

WEEK 41 - LEARN FROM FAILURES

"It's not whether you get knocked down, it's whether you get up." Vince Lombardi

Learning from failures helps to increase your success rate.

The 1 thing

Tip

Understanding the things that did not work, will prevent you from doing the same mistake again.

Space for doodle:

Inspiration

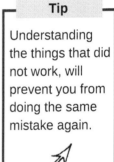

http://bit.ly/tsyfailure

Challenge

Learn from your failures.
What did not work?
Why did it not work?
How can you avoid that
in the future?

List your thoughts here:

Notes:

Your week was

- [ ] sugarfree
- [ ] a feast
- [ ] a green smoothie

Material

Learning from failures worksheet
www.startup-yearbook.com/material

Notes:

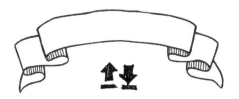

WEEK 42 - LEARN FROM SUCCESSES

"Life is 10% what happens to you and 90% how you react to it." Charles R. Swindoll

Learning from successes is as important as learning from failures.

The 1 thing

···

Tip

Understanding why something succeeded is as important as understanding why it didn't.

···

Inspiration
http://bit.ly/tsysuccess

···

Space for doodle:

Challenge of the week:

What worked? What went well? What was a success? Why was it a success? How can you repeat this success in the future? What transferable things can you define?

....
....
....
....
....
....
....
....
....
....
....
....

Your week was: ☐ a rainbow

☐ a star

☐ a plant

Additional material:
Learn from successes worksheet
www.startup-yearbook.com/material

Space for notes:

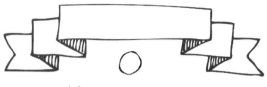

WEEK 43 - BE OPEN-MINDED

"Your reputation is more important than your paycheck, and your integrity is worth more than your career." Ryan Freitas

Being open-minded helps to see new opportunities for your business.

The 1 thing

Tip

In business you need to be open-minded to be able to understand your target group, business partners and suppliers. An open mind will help you to come up with creative ideas to solve issues.

Inspiration

http://bit.ly/tsyopen

Challenge

Is there something that you really don't understand why people do it? What did you used to believe but don't anymore? Try to be open-minded about it. What would happen if you would open up to it?

Your week was

- [ ] a laugh
- [ ] a smile
- [ ] a laugh that was so hard that you almost peed yourself

 Additional material

Worksheet to help you to be more open-minded
www.startup-yearbook.com/material

Space for notes:

WEEK 44 - 80/20 RULE

"If you have more than three priorities, then you don't have any." Jim Collins

Using the 80/20 rule helps you to be more productive.

The 1 thing

Tip

Make use of the Pareto principle — 80/20 rule

Inspiration

http://bit.ly/tsypareto

Challenge: Revisit what you are doing and cut out the 80% that don't get you hardly anything.

List things that don't get you much.

Your week was

☐ a hairdryer

☐ a bath

☐ a toothbrush

Additional material

Explanation of the Pareto principle
www.startup-yearbook.com/material

Space for notes:

WEEK 45 - BE COURAGEOUS

"When you were making excuses someone else was making enterprise." Amit Kalantri

Courage will help you to overcome obstacles.

The 1 thing

Tip

Being an entrepreneur means being courageous. You will face challenges over and over again that you will have to courageously overcome. Establish a courageous work ethic.

Inspiration

http://bit.ly/tsycourage

Space for doodle:

Challenge of the week:

Be courageous. Do one thing this week that is courageous.

List things that you can do to be courageous:

Your week was

☐ King of hearts

☐ Queen of clover

☐ Joker

Additional material:

Inspirational pictures for being courageous
www.startup-yearbook.com/material

Space for notes:

WEEK 46 – STORY TELLING

"Be undeniably good. No marketing effort or social media buzzword can be a substitute for that." Anthony Volodkin

Being able to convey your story helps to connect and be memorable.

The 1 thing

~~~~~~~~~~

Tip: People buy from people. They buy into your story rather than just your products/services.

~~~~~~~~~~

Inspiration
http://bit.ly/tsystory

~~~~~~~~~~

Challenge of the week: Create your story. Why have you started your business? What inspired you to do it?

Space for doodle and other thoughts:

Your week was:

☐ a paintball match

☐ a spa

☐ a walk in the woods

Additional material: More questions to help you writing your story
www.startup-yearbook.com/material

Space for notes:

WEEK 47 - HOW TO PRIORITISE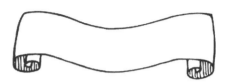

"The last 10% it takes to launch something takes as much energy as the first 90%." Rob Kalin

Knowing how to prioritise helps to be less stressed.

The 1 thing

Tip

Learn how to prioritise in different ways. Try new methods and be surprised by their effectiveness.

Inspiration

http://bit.ly/tsypriority

Challenge

Prioritise and do the one thing that you really don't want to do this week. One thing that is something that you don't like. It will lift a weight off your shoulders.

What don't you want to do?

Your week was

- ☐ pessimistic
- ☐ optimistic
- ☐ sarcastic

Additional material

Ways to prioritise
www.startup-yearbook.com/material

Space for notes

WEEK 48 - SELLING

"Embrace what you don't know, especially in the beginning, because what you don't know can become your greatest asset." Sara Blakely

Selling is a necessary part of your business. Don't ignore it.

The 1 thing

Tip

Working on your business for so long, will have put you into your own bubble. Break out of the bubble to spark innovation.

Inspiration
http://bit.ly/tsysell

Challenge of the week

Try to see your business from a totally different angle. Assume you have never come across a business like yours. What would be your questions? Do you have answers to those questions?

List your questions here:

Your week was:

☐ sleeping in

☐ working late

☐ moving forward

Additional material:
Worksheet to list questions and answers
www.startup-yearbook.com/material

Space for notes

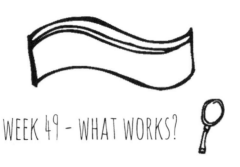

WEEK 49 - WHAT WORKS?

"Learn by doing. Theory is nice, but nothing replaces actual experience." Tony Hsieh

You need to know what works in your business to be successful.

The 1 thing

Tip: You need to keep a critical eye on your business and constantly evaluate what is working and what isn't.

Inspiration
http://bit.ly/tsyevaluate

Challenge of the week:
Write down things that are working in your business. How can you improve these things even further?

Write down things that aren't working in your business. How can you improve them?

Space for doodle:

Your week was
- ☐ a snail
- ☐ a cheetah
- ☐ a dog

Additional material: Worksheet to help you finding out what is working
www.startup-yearbook.com/material

Space for notes:

WEEK 50 - LEARN SOMETHING NEW

"You are never too old to set another goal or to dream a new dream." Les Brown

Learning something new helps to open your mind.

The 1 thing

>————————<

Tip: Learning new things will ensure that your brain is willing to come up with innovative ideas and will improve your memory.

>————————<

Inspiration
http://bit.ly/tsylearn

Challenge of the week:

Pick something new that you would like to learn. A skill, a software, a language, an instrument, anything.

>————————<

Space for doodle:

List things you would like to learn:

Even more space for doodle:

>————————————————————<

Your week was
- [ ] pizza
- [ ] sushi
- [ ] fish & chips

>————————————————————<

Additional material:
Examples of new things to learn
www.startup-yearbook.com/material

>————————————————————<

Space for notes:

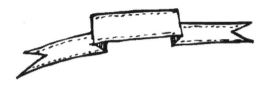

WEEK 51 - YOUR PRODUCTS

"Everything is impossible until somebody does it." Bruce Wayne

Adjusting your products/services for the market will increase sales.

The 1 thing

Tip: Make sure you offer products and services that your target audience actually wants otherwise no one will buy them.

Inspiration
http://bit.ly/tsyreview

Challenge of the week:
Review your products and services.
Do they need adjusting?
Do you need to offer something else?

Write down your thoughts:

Your week was

- ☐ winning the lottery
- ☐ saving money
- ☐ not much at all

Additional material:
Products worksheet
www.startup-yearbook.com/material

Space for notes:

WEEK 52 - THE NEXT YEAR

"Any time is a good time to start a company." Ron Conway

Thinking ahead will make the next year easier.

The 1 thing

 Tip: Review your year and write down the learnings for the coming years. This will help you focus on the important things in business.

Inspiration: http://bit.ly/tsyannualreview

Space for doodle:

Challenge of the week:

Review your year and write down your learnings.

Notes for your review:

Your week was

- [ ] epic
- [ ] a blockbuster
- [ ] a success

Additional material:
Worksheet to review your year
www.startup-yearbook.com/material

Space for notes:

FURTHER SUPPORT

If you would like further support from me, there are many ways to get it. Join the **Creative Start-Up Academy Online Community** in which I run monthly live webinars, challenges, publish FAQ videos, give you book recommendations and support through a forum: www.creativestartupacademy.com/community

Check out the **online courses** – including free ones: www.creativestartupacademy.com/courses

Check out my other **books** that are available on Amazon: 'The Start-Up Formula – 6 easy steps to start your own business' (www.startup-formula.com) and 'The Marketing Formula – 6 steps that will make marketing easy' (www.marketing-formula.com).

Have a look on www.christinethecoach.com for **personal support.**

I am looking forward to connecting with you. All the best for you and your start-up!

Your Marketing and Creative Start-Up Coach – Christine

ABOUT CHRISTINE

I was born and raised in Berlin, Germany and worked in marketing and design agencies for 7 years as a Strategic Consultant and Senior Account Manager.

In 2009, I felt the need for a change. I quit my job, went travelling through New Zealand and Australia before moving to London in 2010. I started a new job as a Senior Account Manager in a design agency.

However, I knew I didn't want to do that for much longer. I was longing for something new, something that would be more rewarding. I trained as a Coach and obtained a certificate in NLP (Neuro Linguistic Programming). Still not knowing exactly what I wanted to do, I called myself a 'Life Coach'. It soon turned out that I enjoy working with other driven individuals that are starting up their own business and following their passions. My purpose in life became clearer: I want to help other people and I want to make them happy in what they do for a living. I became the Marketing and Creative Start-Up Coach.

I now work with universities across Europe to help their start-up students. I work with individuals and small businesses that need help with starting their own business or marketing it successfully. I run regular workshops, give talks about 'starting up and marketing, run boot camps, competitions and work 1:1 with people – in person or via Skype.

I started the Creative Start-Up Academy – an online platform for start-ups and small businesses (www.creativestartupacademy.com).

My passions outside of work are cooking, travelling, Italy (everything about it – language, food, people, and the country itself), dancing salsa and doing exercise. I play the ukulele, which doesn't mean that I can sing, and enjoy spending time with friends, but also with myself.

One of the other exciting projects of I am involved in, is the first Digital Nomad Town in the world: www.digitalnomadtown.com

If you would like to get in contact with me, send me an email: hello@christinethecoach.com

Printed in Poland
by Amazon Fulfillment
Poland Sp. z o.o., Wrocław